IMAGINATION MASTERY:

A WORKBOOK FOR SHIFTING YOUR REALITY

Beca Lewis

Imagination Mastery is published by:
Perception Publishing

This book is part of *the Shift Series*

Original Copyright ©2019 by Beca Lewis

Cover Design: Elizabeth Mackey

The Imagination Mastery Workbook first
Copyright©2019. All rights reserved.

ISBN-13: 978-0-9885520-1-2

Beca's Website: *https://becalewis.com*

Printed in the U.S.A.

WHAT OTHERS SAY ABOUT THIS BOOK

What I found to be especially true and beneficial in this book was working through the exercises, stretch my thinking beyond what the physical senses or limited mind was reporting. I learned that looking forward with good expectations enabled me to find answers even when I had been feeling blocked. Wow. It really isn't my responsibility to figure things out.

I learned how to listen, trust, then act on the angel messages. Since beginning this practice, there are paradigm shifts happening in my day to day experiences that have brought (and continue to bring) measurable healing results, small and large.

I now know and trust that the answers have always been present. Thinking imaginatively has helped me realize my freedom from worry. I am learning to trust that good is all powerful. I am very grateful that I am becoming an Imagination Master! —Barbara Budan

TABLE OF CONTENTS

Author Note:	7
SECTION ONE: WHY IMAGINE	**9**
An Idea 10	
Chapter One: Why Imagine?	12
SECTION TWO: TOOLS	**20**
Chapter Two: Quality Words	**21**
What Are Qualities?	*22*
How To Do A Quality Words List	*24*
How To Use A Quality Words List	*32*
Chapter Three: I Choose	**35**
Let's Choose	*38*
SECTION THREE: THE PRACTICE	**42**
Chapter Four: Imagination	*43*
Chapter Five: Week One	*47*
Week One Set Up	*48*
First Week Review	*58*
First Week I Choose	*60*
First Week Recap	*61*
Chapter Six: Week Two	**63**
Week Two Set Up	*65*
Second Week Review	*75*
Second Week I Choose	*77*
Second Week Recap	*78*
Chapter Seven: Week Three	**80**
Perception Rules	*80*
Week Three Set Up	*86*
Third Week Review	*96*

Third Week I Choose   97
Third Week Recap   100
Chapter Eight: Week Four   **102**
Week Four Set Up   104
Fourth Week Review   114
Fourth Week I Choose   115
Fourth Week Recap   118
Chapter Nine: Week Five   **119**
Week Five Set Up   121
Fifth Week Review   131
Fifth Week I Choose   132
Fifth Week Recap   135
Chapter Ten: Week Six   **136**
Week Six Set Up   139
Sixth Week Review   149
Sixth Week I Choose   150
Sixth Week Recap   153
Chapter Eleven: Week Seven   **155**
Pick Your Symbol   156
Week Seven Set Up   157
Seventh Week Review   167
Seventh Week I Choose   170
Recap   173

AUTHOR NOTE:

When you start to develop your powers of empathy and imagination, the whole world opens up to you. — Susan Sarandon

This book grew out of the *Imagination Mastery* class that I first taught in the spring of 2019.

I wanted to share how imagination, **used in the right way,** can—and does—completely transform our life experiences.

Once the class was over, because I already had most of the worksheets, I thought it would be easy to turn them into an actual book.

I imagined it would be easy. The joke was on me.

It wasn't easy at all, because when I am teaching a class, I am speaking what I want the members of the class to know and do.

To convey the same information in a book means I have to write it. Of course. That's a duh.

But I hadn't realized how many concepts needed explanation until I started writing them out.

That meant I had to write this book in a different style than most of my other books.

I wrote it as if I was teaching the *Imagination Mastery* class, and you, my reader was in that class.

In my mind's eye, I am with you as you read this book and work through the lessons.

As you read this book you'll see there are a lot of worksheets.

If you would prefer to not write in the book I have a **free** download of a PDF version of just the worksheets for you. No other writing. Just the worksheets.

You can follow along in the book. You can either print them out or write on them on your computer.

Even if you are reading a hard copy of the book, and the worksheets are in it, you might still want those worksheets, so you don't have to write in the book.

That way, you can do the exercises over and over again.

Find those worksheets and how to contact me here: becalewis.com/imagination

I would love to hear what happens, and what works for you.

Imagining with you, ~ Beca

SECTION ONE: WHY IMAGINE

An Idea

Before you begin...

This course is a fantastic one to do with a group of friends or a mastermind group.

Even one other person would be great.

You'll keep each other on track and accountable, something that we all need. Besides, later on, there will be an exercise to do that is best with a partner.

If you can, find someone, or a group of people, **that have your best interests in mind.** People who have the same desires as you to shift their life, and who you trust to keep your "secrets."

Don't think you know anyone like this? Don't worry!

Do the course on your own, knowing that it will help you find those people.

Because like-minded, like-souled, people do find each other when the time is right.

If you need help, let me know.

There might be a group going on that you can join, or I could be teaching a live class just as you begin this. Find me at becalewis.com.

For now, though, don't wait. Get started.

Things will shift to bring you what you need and want if you are faithful to the practice and to yourself.

CHAPTER ONE: WHY IMAGINE?

The man who has no imagination has no wings. — Muhammad Ali

Here is the question you might, and probably should be, asking yourself.

Why bother with learning how to be an Imagination Master? What practical use could being a master of imagination be in the "real" world, or daily life?

Perhaps you are wondering why you would waste the next few months of your life practicing how to imagine.

I mean, after all, what will your friends and family say? Perhaps they would ask you if there aren't more productive ways to spend your time.

And then there is always the chance that, like me, imagining is something you were supposed to stop doing. Or at least hide that you are doing it.

I can't tell you how many times a teacher, or parent, would catch me staring into space and ask me, "Are you daydreaming again?"

Yes. Yes, I was, and it was fun!

After all, I was a reader of fairy tales and science

fiction, and it all seemed so marvelous. It seemed so much better than sitting behind a desk in a square room.

I asked myself what it would be like if I were a fairy in the forest? Or if there was a unicorn waiting for me to ride home.

They were the imaginations of a little girl. What good were those imaginations to me, other than to make life more fun?

And what good will being a master of imagination be for you, or me, as an adult?

Sure, now that I am long past grown-up, I can turn my imaginations into stories, and then books, and that seems like a practical thing to do after all.

But that is only one small use for it. It doesn't answer the question of why you, or I, would want to be an Imagination Master at any age over ten.

There is such a good reason that it is almost shocking.

Especially since we have been taught that the world is only what we see or experience through our five senses. That we need to grow up and make a living. That success can be measured.

What if that was all wrong?

Imagine this. It is!

Imagination is actually where our future lives. Imagination is what creates inventions that make our lives better.

Imagination brought us Einstein's equations, airplanes, the internet, electric lights, the smartphone, and countless other inventions that have changed our life.

Imagination had us take a chance on love, on finding friends that don't look like us and visit the moon. All because of imagination.

But there is still more than that.

And it's all because of this:

"The Subconscious mind can not tell the difference between what's real and what's imagined." — Bob Proctor

Think about this, and you'll know it's true.

Have you ever watched something on TV and started to laugh, cry, or feel afraid?

Have you ever cried because you heard a sad story? It had nothing to do with you, but you felt it?

Have you ever worried over something that never happened? Been afraid, and then discovered that what you were afraid of was a story someone made up?

Yes, you have. We all have. That is imagination at work.

Our minds, our subconscious minds, our rational minds, do not know the difference between reality and imagination.

Even our memories are not accurate. We have re-imagined the past in a way that works for us.

The horror of that moment," the King went on, "I shall never never forget!"
"You will, though," the Queen said, "if you don't make a memorandum of it.
—The White King and Queen, *Through the Looking Class* by Lewis Carroll

Imagine that. Imagine what that means! It means we could imagine what we want to be real. We can rewrite the story of our lives, any time that we want to.

Wait? What?

Yes. It's true. So why don't we use imagination more often to design how we want to live?

John Kennedy, in his famous speech on May 25, 1961, dared us to dream of going to the moon. He used a trick in that speech to get us to imagine it. Over and over again, he repeated the phrase, "We choose to go to the moon."

What was he doing? **He was reprogramming the nation's belief system.** We all imagined what going to the moon would look like. But most of all, we imagined what it would *feel* like.

And what happened? We went to the moon.

Many people say that John Kennedy's death was a turning point in our world. What would our world be like if he kept on forcing us to imagine a better future for all humankind?

It's probably why mourning for him has lasted so long. We mourn for what could have been.

He can't imagine a better future for all of the earth anymore, but we can.

The subconscious mind is far more powerful than the conscious mind. But it will stay in pre-programmed ruts and direct our lives without our knowledge unless we learn to change it. Expand it. Use it to reveal a reality that works.

How do we do that?

We become Imagination Masters, again. Because we already are, or were, as children. It's time to get back to it—on purpose.

What you perceive to be reality magnifies.

That's just the way it is. So let's imagine.

However, in this book, we are not going imagine, or visualize, what we already know.

We are **not** going to turn our daily imaginations into either an "I want this" or a "to-do" list.

No. We are going to do so much more.

We are going to imagine what we don't know— what we haven't seen before. Ride moonbeams. Summon a magic carpet and visit the fairies who used to live in our backyard.

What good will this do? It will turn on the spigot to new ideas and a new reality. In more practical terms, it creates new neural pathways in our brains. Everything gets easier, brighter, more fun, more successful.

Less discord. More imagination.

As humans, we are spectacularly good at imagining the "what if" scenarios of disaster, or ill health, or worry-filled days.

Stop it! Not just because it is a waste of time, but because that is creating a reality for you to experience, and is that the one you want?

Instead, think "what if" and imagine glorious things. Good things. For you, and everyone.

Don't make it happen. Imagine it. Step back. Feel what it would be like if it were true.

Then imagine again.

That's what we are going to do together for seven weeks.

Perhaps when you've finished, you will do it again, until imagination becomes what drives your day.

Imagine a different way to solve a problem, to speak a hard truth to a friend, or heal an illness.

Have I convinced you of the value of taking just a few minutes out of your day, every day, to become better at the one thing that can change everything?

If not, convince yourself. Give it a try.

IMAGINATION. NOT VISUALIZATION

One more thing, before you begin.

Imagination is not visualization. This is not a book called Visualization Mastery for a good reason. They are two different things.

Visualization is an excellent tool when we are working on something we want to make better. There are many studies about how visualization improves everything from golf games, to performing better on stage.

*Imagination is **outside of** what we already know.*

When we imagine, we take ourselves out of the world as we know it.

We are not trying to make things better by visualizing them. We are not trying to get something by visualizing.

We are imagining because within our small limited viewpoint of the world we are missing most of what is really going on.

By imagining, we'll begin to see more, experience more, and it will be greater than we could ever have visualized.

Have fun with it. Don't be serious. Be childlike. Imagine, the best, most amazing—whatever—that you can. It will only get better as the days go by.

Let's get started.

I'll see you on the other side.

SECTION TWO: TOOLS

Chapter Two: Quality Words

Imagination should be used, not to escape reality, but to create it. —Colin Wilson

Shall we begin? Let's create a new reality together. But first, let's talk about a few of the essential tools that you will be using in this course.

There are two of them that you might not have ever done before, or at least the way that we will be using them. So, let's take a moment and talk about what they are and how to use them.

Quality Lists and I Choose sheets.

These two tools are invaluable, so don't skip them!

Let's start with quality words.

I know you know that thoughts are things, but using the concept of quality words, we are going to work backwards to that idea.

We are going to find the qualities of things, first, and then translate them back into things.

That means that the "things" in your life will more accurately reflect what you want after using this tool.

This includes everything from the shoes you are wearing to the people that you love.

Yes, I know people are not a "thing," but they are a set of qualities, like everything that we see and experience.

However, to get us started, we won't start with people. We'll begin with easier things, like birds, trees, stones, flowers, and animals.

After that, people will be much easier to translate into qualities. Well, everything will be. You'll see.

After a while, I hope that you will get into the habit of using quality words all the time, especially when you are looking for ways to make a decision or a shift in your life.

I promise that their use will make changes much easier, and the outcome more in alignment with what you desire.

However, for now, you are going to use them in your Imagination Mastery work and begcome an expert at using them.

WHAT ARE QUALITIES?

Here's what they are not.

Quality words are not sentences.

If you find yourself having to write a sentence, or even a few words, to describe what you see or feel, you haven't hit the quality yet.

Keep listening within, and trust what you hear. You can always change your mind.

Remember, we are translating things back to thoughts, which is where they originate. If we shift our thoughts and beliefs, the "thing" has to respond to that shift.

Here's what quality words are.

Quality words describe in one word the essence of something.

You'll discover as we go along how important these words become. It takes a bit of practice, but after using this idea for a few weeks, it will make so much sense you'll wonder how you got along without them before.

By the way, there are no right or wrongs with what words you choose.

You don't have to explain what the words mean to anyone, including yourself.

In fact, please don't. Qualities are a feeling, an emotion, an intuition, an inner knowing. These things can't be described, and there is no need to do so.

The quality word is a place marker for all that it represents.

If you are working with a friend or mastermind group to do this course, go ahead and share your quality words.

However, don't try to describe them. Let them exist on their own. And don't suggest words to each other.

Discover them by working together, not by one person knowing more than someone else.

Your quality words are personal as are theirs. No corrections are necessary unless they come from within yourself.

How To Do A Quality Words List

Why do we complete a list of quality words after every week of imagining?

Because all that we want, or imagine, has to be **translated back** into what it really means to us.

Doing this means we will stop wasting time searching for material things to make us happy.

Using quality words, we will discover what we truly want.

Often we'll find we already have it. We simply didn't recognize it because we were looking for the wrong thing.

All things are, in essence, composed of qualities.

When we translate things back into their qualities, a fantastic thing happens. We become conscious of what is already present for us. It may not look like we thought it was going to look, but it will be what we wanted.

But first, we have to find out what our heart wants.

Quality words will become a way of life once you experience the power of them. So, let's get started and make you an expert at using quality words to shift your life.

Here are the steps:

Step 1: Take a moment and list 8 to 10 qualities of something you want to see, or experience.

Remember, use one word to express each quality. If you are using sentences, you have not come to the heart of it.

Step 2: There are two kinds of quality lists: You can either list the qualities of what the thing looks like, or you can list the qualities of how you will feel when you have it.

For example, buying a car.

Your quality list for the thing—or car—might contain ideas such as red, fast, inexpensive, safe, etc.

If you choose to make a quality list of how you will *feel* when you drive this car, it might read "wealthy, secure, free, joyful, etc."

For this Imagination Mastery course, you will be using the lists you will make at the end of each week.

Step 3: Now that you have the quality list, the next step is to put these qualities in order. Why is this important?

Have you ever been at a place in your life where nothing happens towards what you want no matter what you do?

This is most likely because you have a quality or value block.

If you have two values that feel equal to you, your core-self will be confused as to which one to provide.

Continuing with the car example, let's say you list the qualities of luxury and frugal. Until you know which quality is first, you'll be stuck, and nothing will happen.

This is because at first glance they appear to be

conflicting.

However, once your list is in order, you can receive, or see, all of what you have listed, because in an unlimited big R Reality, everything has already been provided for you under the law of God's Grace.

CRITICAL NEXT STEP

You need help to put the list in order!

Doing this is critical and that is why having a partner while doing this course would be very helpful.

Someone else needs to help you put them in the order that your intuition, heart, internal voice, guidance, wants them to be.

This order *will not be the same order* that your intellectual mind put them in while making the list.

Don't look at your list while this person is working with you, as this will engage brain and logic.

What you want to engage is your heart and inspiration.

The person with your list will ask you the following question:

"Which is more important to you?" and will

give you two words on the list to compare.

The person *must not* give you any other verbal or physical cues. *Don't listen to anything except your inner voice.* Respond with the answer it tells you. Don't argue with it.

If you are unable to choose one as more important than the other, the person should ask you, "Which one can you not live without?"

Notice that your mind tells you that if you choose one, you might not get the other.

That fear is coming from the point of view that there is never enough and that you don't deserve everything you want.

Since neither statement is true, notice these thoughts and move on. The truth is, once you are clear about what you desire to see, you will be able to see and receive all these qualities, in a form that is appropriate for you.

Each word **must be compared with every word** until you have an ordered list. You will probably be surprised at the order if you have stayed with your heart and trusted your answers.

Here is how I do this.

(Don't worry, this is a step-by-step process. Not hard. Don't let worry get in the way.)

Take a sheet of paper. Draw a line down the middle. Write the quality words on the left.

Put your finger on the first word on your partner's list. (This is so you don't lose your place.)

Ask the "which is more important" question comparing the first word on the list to the second one.

If they say the first word, move on to comparing the first word to the third word.

What if they say the second word is more important? Great.

Cross it off and move it to the right side of the page.

Now compare the first word to the third word. If they say the first word is more important, move on.

What if they say the third word is more important than the first? Great. Cross it off.

But before you move it to the right side of the page, you have to find out if it is more important, or less important than the word that is already over there.

To do that, ask the "which is more important" question between those two words on the right.

Let's say the third word is more important than

the second, so write it above the second word.

Go back to the left side of the list.

Your finger is still on that first word. Compare it to the fourth word, and so on down the list until you have done the entire left side of the list.

If you have found more words that are more important than the first one, they will go to the right side after you compare them to that list, from the bottom up.

For example:

You have two words on the right. The third word is first, and then the second.

Now you have a new word. Compare it to the second. If it is more important, compare it to the third. If it is more important, put it at the top, if it isn't, it goes in the middle.

(Here's where you realize you need lots of spaces between the words on the right because you never know where the list is going.)

After you have completed comparing the first word all the way down the list on the left, you will have some crossed-out words on the left, because they are now on the right in their right order.

Cross out the first word, and add it at the bottom of the list on the right.

Draw a line under that list. You are done with those words.

Go to the list on the left. Put your finger on the first uncrossed out word. Compare it with the next uncrossed out word below it.

Do the same thing with the words that you did before.

When you are done doing that with the new words, put a line under the list and start again on the left.

Usually, this is done in two or three passes. But keep going until all the words are crossed out on the left and in order on the list on the right.

Now you can move to how to use this list.

Remember, you can't ask yourself these questions. Otherwise, you will answer the question with the same mind that made it, the intellectual mind.

We need the heart, gut, intuitive mind answering to get the list in the correct order.

Even if you don't have a friend doing this course with you, you can still hand someone this "how to do this" information and let them walk you through your list.

If you need a visual of this, there is a video of a friend doing this on the same page where you will get your worksheets:
becalewis.com/imaginationimagination

How To Use A Quality Words List

Now that you have a quality word list, how do you use it? Of course, you could ignore it and hope things change. But now that you have put so much work into the list why not make the most of it?

Here are the four simple ways to use your list. Use it and get ready to experience more than you might imagine.

1. Use the qualities as a filter.

If something appears that you think might be what you are looking for **and does not have at least the first four qualities**—with the first one first and the rest following in order, it is not "it!"

Think of the time you will save if you can eliminate quickly and easily what is not right for you.

For example, you discover that safety is first on your quality list for a means of transportation and the car you are looking at has a very low safety record, don't buy this car no matter how much you love it.

If you buy it, you will eventually be unhappy with it, and somehow you will unconsciously figure out how to get rid of it.

2. See the qualities everywhere.

See the qualities in everything, not just in what you're seeking. Notice that they're always with you in many forms.

You have always had, and always will have, each quality on your list if you practice looking and expect to see it.

A quality does not have to belong to you. It can appear anywhere. **All of what you see is your world.** The goal is to notice that the quality you're looking for already exists everywhere, and since you can see it—it exists for you—now.

3. Be grateful for each quality as you see it.

Be grateful for these qualities each time you see them, no matter where they occur. If the person you dislike most has one of these qualities, be grateful that you have seen this quality in your life.

Know that if it is "out there" it was first "within here" and therefore always available, and always part of your life.

4. Be and live these qualities yourself.

Now that you have begun to live with these qualities I know that you are discovering that having the "thing" you wanted is no longer as important.

You have found that It already exists as thoughts—qualities.

As we express gratitude for this fact, we are living within Grace.

The result?

Sometimes we realize we don't actually need the thing we were asking to see, or it turns up in another package, or it appears in a way more excellent than we could have dreamed.

Whichever way this happens, you have begun by seeking the essence of the "thing" that you want. That beginning cannot help but produce in your world whatever you need at the moment. You have always had it.

None of us have ever been abandoned, nor could we ever be. Looking for qualities opens our eyes to what has always been and always will be ours.

That changes everything.

CHAPTER THREE: I CHOOSE

I choose, therefore I am.
—Amit Goswami, The Self-Aware Universe

I wanted to change the world. But I found that the only thing one can be sure of changing is oneself.
—Aldous Huxley

We choose to go to the moon. We choose to go to the moon in this decade and do the other things, not because they are easy, but because they are hard, because that goal will serve to organize and measure the best of our energies and skills, because that challenge is one that we are willing to accept, one we are unwilling to postpone, and one which we intend to win, and the others, too.—John F. Kennedy

At the end of each week, I have included a chance to do an *I Choose* sheet. If you feel no resistance at all to what you have discovered you want, then you could skip this step.

However, that is not likely, is it?

It is our resistance that keeps us stuck.

Sometimes that resistance is so apparent we are well aware of it. Other times, it hides in the shadows, and we only know it's there because of the symptoms of lethargy, anger, and discouragement, to name a few.

I could spend a long time talking about resistance, but instead let me send you to Steven Pressfield's book, *The War Of Art*.

Although he is talking about resistance in terms of an artist, it applies to every one of us, all the time.

So, let's assume that you have some resistance to living a better life, whether it is buried or noticeable.

Doing this extremely simple-to-do *I Choose* exercise works what others might call miracles.

One of those miracles happened to me many years ago. My husband had left and I had no idea that was going to happen. I came home from a trip and he was gone.

I had no idea what to do. All my get up and go, had got up and left, too.

I was struggling to pay bills, feed my family, and support a home that I had just purchased.

I loved that house. I can still walk through it in my mind and tell you everything that was there because I designed the whole thing to be exactly how I wanted it to be.

I knew that I needed to sell it because I couldn't afford the payments, but I resisted that idea until one day my oldest daughter, who was in her last year of high school said, "Mom. Sell the house. You have no other choice."

I knew she was right. I had to do it. So I put into practice all the things that we are talking about in this book.

I gathered a small group of people I knew, loved, and trusted who also had some difficult decisions to make.

We formed what we called a flash mastermind group with the express intention of doing what we had been resisting, and doing it quickly.

We made *Quality Lists*, and *I Choose* sheets. I did *I Choose* sheets every moment I had a chance to write. I sat in meetings and wrote them instead of taking notes. I covered sheets and sheets of paper.

Our flash mastermind group disbanded a month later after meeting only four times. We had all completed the task we had been resisting.

For me, my house sold at a higher price than my Realtor thought was possible. It was the first offer, and it was for cash.

I never looked at those sheets after I wrote them out. There was no reason to rehash old thoughts.

It would have been like looking through the garbage.

Have I convinced you to try this out?

Consciously choosing will allow your life to unfold effortlessly.

We set ourselves up to fail in most of our choices or resolutions because we don't stop and listen to the monkey voice's response to the choice.

It always resists. **Always**. So unless we deal with our resistance, we struggle more than necessary.

Let's Choose

At the end of each week in this book, you will have already set up what you want to choose. Using an *I Choose* sheet will move it forward.

Here's an example of what that might look like using an example that I think most people will relate to.

Begin by stating what you want as a choice.

Say this: *I choose to have a good-looking and healthy body.*

Now stop and listen!

Perhaps the voice says:

"Ha, well sure you may want to have this body, but you will have to exercise to get it."

Respond something like this:

I choose to exercise.

Listen again. Perhaps the voice says:

"You hate to exercise."

Respond:

I choose to love to exercise.

Listen again. The voice may say:

"You don't have the time to exercise."

Respond:

I choose to have the time to exercise.

The voice:

"You don't have anything to wear to exercise."

Respond:

I choose to have something to wear to exercise.

See how this works?

The list can, and probably will, run on for a page or two for just one simple choice.

Some of mine have gone on for days and days

filling multiple sheets of paper.

What we are doing by choosing consciously is uncovering, without attachment and emotion, all the hidden choices and beliefs that have kept us from actually doing the thing we thought we had resolved to do. We are shifting our perception.

If you are doing this *Imagination Mastery* workbook with someone, share what you have chosen.

Then watch each other to make sure that you don't do or say things that contradict what you have chosen. You will become protectors of each other's dreams.

Remember, you can never consciously choose too often.

I have a choice in every moment to keep my heart open or closed, to live in love or fear. More than any other specific practice, I have found that maintaining the awareness of choice is the most important factor in keeping an open heart, for every action, every thought, every moment contains the potential for bringing us closer to either intimacy and healing or isolation and suffering.
—Dean Ornish, M.D., Love and Survival: The Scientific Basis for the Healing Power of Intimacy

There is a vitality, a life force, a quickening that is translated through you into action, and there is only one of you in all time, this expression is unique, and if you block it, it will never exist through any other medium; and be lost.

The world will not have it. It is not your business to determine how good it is, nor how it compares with other expression. It is your business to keep it yours clearly and directly, to keep the channel open.

You do not even have to believe in yourself or your work. You have to keep open and aware directly to the urges that motivate you. Keep the channel open. No artist is pleased.

There is no satisfaction whatever at any time. There is a queer, divine dissatisfaction, a blessed unrest that keeps us marching and makes us more alive than the others.
—Martha Graham

Unless this thing is consistent with the highest right, I do not want it; and if it is, I can trust God's law to establish it.
—The Lord Thy Confidence (pamphlet from 1912)

SECTION THREE: THE PRACTICE

CHAPTER FOUR: IMAGINATION

Your imagination is everything. It is the preview of life's coming attractions. —Albert Einstein

Now that you have the basic tools, are you ready to get started?

Each week has a different focus, but the imagination exercises each day will remain mostly the same.

Try not to get behind, but if you do, it's okay.

This is not a race. The turtle always wins because it stays focused.

If you get your rational mind out of the way when you start these exercises, you can complete each day's assignment within five to ten minutes.

Don't worry. Let go. Imagine.

Be like the White Queen!

"I can't believe that!" said Alice.
"Can't you?" the Queen said in a pitying tone.
"Try again: draw a long breath, and shut your eyes."
Alice laughed. "There's no use trying," she said:
"one can't believe impossible things."
"I daresay you haven't had much practice," said the Queen. "When I was your age, I always did it for half-

an-hour a day. Why, sometimes I've believed as many as six impossible things before breakfast."

Every day we are going to be like the White Queen. She was quite the Imagination Master, wasn't she?

She was continuously trying to get Alice to become an Imagination Master, too. In this passage from Alice In Wonderland, the White Queen gives Alice a task.

Imagine six impossible things before breakfast.

So we are going to follow her advice but do it differently.

We are going to imagine seven impossible things every day for the next seven weeks.

Except, it doesn't have to be before breakfast, or even all at one time.

You can fill out your daily imagination forms as you go through your day, or all at once. Whichever way works best for you.

Personally, I like to sit down first thing in the morning and write out everything that comes to mind. When I allow my thoughts to flow, not judge them, I can complete this assignment within five minutes.

Perhaps it will take you longer at first, but pay

attention. Is that part of yourself being like Alice and saying, "I can't believe that."

Remember we are not trying to be rational or use our intelligence, we are imagining!

By the way, here's how you can tell if you are in your rational mind as you do this.

When what you are writing doesn't feel impossible. Or it feels as if everything you imagine is stupid. Or silly. Or a waste of time.

Come on, let go.

Just for a few minutes a day, in the safety of your own life, imagine that life is full of glories, possibilities, that are entirely invisible to the rational mind.

Be irrational. Imagine what that will feel like. Be free!

Why seven impossible things, instead of six?

Because, years ago, when I first started teaching this exercise, everyone liked the number seven better.
It's a number that represents completion, so we are going with that!

Why imagine yourself as all the different kinds of beings that we are going to imagine ourselves to be each week?

Because we aren't birds, trees, animals, stone or flowers, therefore, we don't have preconceived notions about what it would be like to be one.

It's an all-new experience. It's out of our rational, controlling mind.

This workbook is all about expanding our imagination. We are going beyond what is evident to the senses so that we can break out of ruts and stuck places.

Don't fight it. Go with it.

By the end of this book, if you have done the work, all your questions about "why" will be answered.

Not by me, but by you and what you have discovered.

Go boldly where you have never gone before. Imagination. It's the final frontier!

It's where everything changes.

CHAPTER FIVE: WEEK ONE

Imagination is more important than knowledge.
Knowledge is limited. Imagination encircles the world.
—Albert Einstein

Let's start our first week of imagining with these beautiful citizens of the sky—our bird friends.

Yes, this week you are going to imagine that you are a bird.

Maybe you know birds. Perhaps you don't pay any attention to them.

None of that matters in imagination.

Be the bird that arrived in your mind. **The one you just thought of as you read this.** Take that one. It has a message for you.

Don't bother telling me that no bird popped into your mind. One did. Accept it. Go with it.

Still, don't know what bird? Don't try to figure it out. If you are stuck, imagine that a bird did choose you. See. That worked.

This process will be correct for each week as we imagine ourselves to be something we are not, from birds, trees, stones, or flowers.

They will choose you. Let that happen.

Remember you are doing this to break out of what you have been doing all your lives.

Only then can you move into a new version of life, a better one. One that exists beyond our imagination right now. You are going to change that.

Ready to leap? Let's go!

WEEK ONE SET UP

Live out of your imagination, not your history.
—Stephen R. Covey

Today's Date:_____

Remember: **Do not try to figure this out!**

Allow the divine, the creative force, imagination, to move your pencil.

Play with the idea of being your bird. What does it feel like? You can fly this week. Where are you flying to? What is your home like? What song do you sing?

This week I imagine myself to be this bird:_____

How would you feel if you were this bird? Listen within to hear the answers. Try for ten qualities! (This is your unordered quality words list.)

1._____

2._____

3. _____

4. _____

5. _____

6. _____

7. _____

8. _____

9. _____

10. _____

My bird looks like this to me: (Go ahead. Draw, paste, scribble, your bird. No, it doesn't have to look like it. Don't judge, Play!)

Check back to *Chapter Two* on Quality Lists to remind yourself how to put these words in order and then how to use them.

My quality words in order for how I would feel if I were this bird.

1._____

2._____

3. _____

4. _____

5. _____

6. _____

7. _____

8. _____

9. _____

10. _____

Fantastic! Now that you have these qualities— use them. Imagine yourself as this bird this week instead of your ordinary self. Let this bird help you do your daily imaginations.

WEEK ONE: DAY ONE

Today's Date:_____

My Seven Impossible Things Before Breakfast.

1._____
_____

2._____
_____

3._____
_____

4._____
_____

5._____
_____

6._____
_____

7._____
_____

WEEK ONE: DAY TWO

Today's Date:_____

My Seven Impossible Things Before Breakfast.

1._____
_____

2._____
_____

3._____
_____

4._____
_____

5._____
_____

6._____
_____

7._____
_____

WEEK ONE: DAY THREE

Today's Date:_____

My Seven Impossible Things Before Breakfast

1._____
_____

2._____
_____

3._____
_____

4._____
_____

5._____
_____

6._____
_____

7._____
_____

WEEK ONE: DAY FOUR

Today's Date:_____

My Seven Impossible Things Before Breakfast

1._____
_____

2._____
_____

3._____
_____

4._____
_____

5._____
_____

6._____
_____

7._____
_____

WEEK ONE: DAY FIVE

Today's Date:_____

My Seven Impossible Things Before Breakfast

1._____
_____

2._____
_____

3._____
_____

4._____
_____

5._____
_____

6._____
_____

7._____
_____

WEEK ONE: DAY SIX

Today's Date:_____

My Seven Impossible Things Before Breakfast

1._____
_____

2._____
_____

3._____
_____

4._____
_____

5._____
_____

6._____
_____

7._____
_____

WEEK ONE: DAY SEVEN

Today's Date:_____

My Seven Impossible Things Before Breakfast

1._____
_____

2._____
_____

3._____
_____

4._____
_____

5._____
_____

6._____
_____

7._____
_____

First Week Review

The world is but a canvas to the imagination.
—Henry David Thoreau

Now that this first week is over, it's time to review what happened.

First, look over all the impossible things that you wrote. You have forty-nine of them to pick from, a treasure trove of abundance!

Did you do some more than once? Don't worry. Don't judge. That's just what happened.

Go ahead, pick the one you like the most and write it below. Can't decide? Just pick one. You can't go wrong.

Then spend a few minutes to write about it.

Again, I'll say it over and over again. Don't judge. This isn't a writing contest.

No one will see it but you. Write it the way you want to. The important part is putting pen to paper and letting go.

What's happening here? We are training ourselves to be aware of what we are thinking and doing.

No matter how aware we might think we are, there is always room for improvement.

If you discover that you aren't aware? That's good news, too. It means you will experience the joys of awareness to an even greater extent as we travel through imagination together.

My Favorite Impossible Thing For The Week:

_____
_____
_____
_____
_____

Things I noticed:

_____
_____
_____
_____

What has changed?

_____
_____
_____
_____
_____
_____
_____
_____

First Week I Choose

Imagination will often carry us to worlds that never were. But without it we go nowhere.—Carl Sagan

Take one of your impossible things, perhaps your favorite one, choose it, and use it to do this exercise.

No matter how far "out there" it may be, use it anyway.

In this exercise, we are stretching out our minds just as we do our bodies. We can't get past our habits by staying in the same mindset.

I Choose sheets are another vital tool for being mentally flexible.

Remind yourself how to do this by reviewing *Chapter Three*, the *I Choose* chapter in this workbook. Have fun with this!

(This might be where you grab a piece of scrap paper and start writing. It's possible this could go on for pages!)

I Choose This Impossible Thing:

_____

_____

_____

First Week Recap

If you did the work this week, you might be surprised by what happened. And imagine this, you have only just begun.

(If you haven't done it yet, don't fret. You can do it now!)

Here is what you have done this week.

•You spent seven days imagining seven impossible things. You made a quality list of what you would feel like if you were the bird that picked you.

•You chose your favorite imagination, thought about it, commented on it, and did an I Choose sheet, using it as a jumping-off point.

Did you notice that sometimes your daily assignment took only a few minutes a day?

Sometimes it took much longer. Neither is right or wrong.

This imagination work is not about how much time it takes to get it done, but overcoming the resistance to doing it.

When you run across resistance, tell it to go outside and play and leave you alone.

This is the most important kind of work you can do every today because it will make everything else easy, or unnecessary, and definitely more expansive.

Here are some quick "tricks" you can use to defeat that resistance.

• Don't judge how or what you write.
• Don't question it.
• Do follow the internal voice that is guiding you.
• Don't try to make it important.
• Don't try to write something to make it happen.
• Do let go.
• Do allow yourself to be delighted.

Yes! You can have more than seven imaginations a day. Seven primes the pump.

If your imagination starts to flow, go with it!

This entire workbook is designed to get the imagination juices going. If the flow of creativity starts acting like a raging river, grab a raft, and hang on for the ride of your life.

On the other hand, a quick reflection pool could be the perfect place to hang out.

Wherever you find yourself, be grateful. You have the ability to imagine. That in itself is a gift.

Reality is for people that lack imagination.
—Hayao Miyazak

CHAPTER SIX: WEEK TWO

Imagination is the true magic carpet.
—Norman Vincent Peale

Welcome to your second week of Imagination Mastery!

Just as the benefits of consistently doing any exercise changes you, so will doing these imagination exercises.

As with all exercise, sometimes the results are immediately noticeable.

Other times we have to wait patiently and trust that what we are doing is working. But always, always, there will be results when we do the work.

With that in mind, shall we get started?

PICK YOUR SYMBOL

This week you are going to pick a tree, or you are going to allow a tree to choose you.

Stop a second. Even if you don't know the name of the tree that popped into your heart, choose it.

Take time to learn more about your tree this week. What's its official name? How does it grow?

Allow the tree to give you messages that you can apply to your own life.

Perhaps your bird from last week visits your tree. What do they teach and share with each other, and with you?

ADDING SOMETHING NEW

We are adding something else to your morning routine. Meditation.

To be more specific, *imagination meditation.*

Try to spend at least fifteen minutes every day and let yourself *feel* an imagination. It doesn't matter which one of your imaginations that you choose, anyone will do. None are more important than others.

Or imagine yourself to be a tree or your bird. What would that be like to live as a tree or a bird?

As you do your imagination exercises this week, don't try to make something happen, don't wish you were better than you are at imagination, don't want what you imagine to be important.

Nothing is more important than another. Everything counts equally.

Just let go.

For your meditation, find someplace quiet, and feels safe to you. Let the thoughts go by without trying to do anything about them. Allow yourself to drop into your feelings.

Enjoy this time. It will feel delightful once you get the hang of it. Don't cheat yourself by leaving this out of your day. Even if you end up having only two minutes, take those.

Remember, as always, no judgment—starting with yourself.

WEEK TWO SET UP

Everything you can imagine is real.
—Pablo Picasso

Today's Date:_____

Play with the idea of being your tree.

What does it feel like? This week you stay in one place. Or do you? Maybe you have a magical tree that walks. It at least sways. Trees feed and care for the entire world. Look up the symbol of your tree, how does that relate to you?

This week I imagine myself to be this tree:_____

How would you feel if you were this tree? Listen within to hear the answers. Try for ten qualities! (This is your unordered quality words list.)

1._____

2._____

3. _____

4. _____

5. _____

6. _____

7. _____

8. _____

9. _____

10. _____

My tree looks like this to me: (Go ahead. Draw, paste, scribble, your tree. No, it doesn't have to look like it. Don't judge, Play!)

Check back to *Chapter Two* on Quality Lists to remind yourself how to put these words in order and then how to use them.

My quality words in order for how I would feel if I were this tree.

1._____

2._____

3. _____

4. _____

5. _____

6. _____

7. _____

8. _____

9. _____

10. _____

Fantastic! Now that you have these qualities— use them. Imagine yourself as this tree this week instead of your ordinary self. Let this tree help you do your daily imaginations.

WEEK TWO: DAY ONE

Today's Date:_____

Today's Meditation Focus:_____

My Seven Impossible Things Before Breakfast.

1._____
_____

2._____
_____

3._____
_____

4._____
_____

5._____
_____

6._____
_____

7._____
_____

WEEK TWO: DAY TWO

Today's Date:_____

Today's Meditation Focus:_____

My Seven Impossible Things Before Breakfast.

1._____
_____

2._____
_____

3._____
_____

4._____
_____

5._____
_____

6._____
_____

7._____
_____

WEEK TWO: DAY THREE

Today's Date:_____

Today's Meditation Focus:_____

My Seven Impossible Things Before Breakfast.

1._____
_____

2._____
_____

3._____
_____

4._____
_____

5._____
_____

6._____
_____

7._____
_____

WEEK TWO: DAY FOUR

Today's Date:_____

Today's Meditation Focus:_____

My Seven Impossible Things Before Breakfast.

1._____
_____

2._____
_____

3._____
_____

4._____
_____

5._____
_____

6._____
_____

7._____
_____

Week Two: Day Five

Today's Date:_____

Today's Meditation Focus:_____

My Seven Impossible Things Before Breakfast.

1._____
_____

2._____
_____

3._____
_____

4._____
_____

5._____
_____

6._____
_____

7._____
_____

Week Two: Day Six

Today's Date:_____

Today's Meditation Focus:_____

My Seven Impossible Things Before Breakfast.

1._____
_____

2._____
_____

3._____
_____

4._____
_____

5._____
_____

6._____
_____

7._____
_____

WEEK TWO: DAY SEVEN

Today's Date:_____

Today's Meditation Focus:_____

My Seven Impossible Things Before Breakfast.

1._____
_____

2._____
_____

3._____
_____

4._____
_____

5._____
_____

6._____
_____

7._____
_____

SECOND WEEK REVIEW

You need imagination in order to imagine a future that doesn't exist. —Azar Nafisi

Two weeks of imagining!

Can you feel your imagination muscle getting stronger? Are some of your old viewpoints beginning to dissolve?

Did anything happen that surprised you this week?

What happened during your meditations?

Just make a note of it, but don't worry about what happened. Or even celebrate it. Because it will always be different, and it will always be perfect for the day.

Now is the time to pick one of your favorite imaginations and write about it. Why it's your favorite doesn't matter. What and how you write doesn't matter.

Remember what we are doing is training ourselves to be aware of what we are thinking and doing. And then we are allowing our imaginations to bring us into unlimited possibilities.

Doing this is not work. It is a celebration!

My Favorite Impossible Thing For The Week:

_____
_____
_____
_____
_____

Things I noticed:

_____
_____
_____
_____

What has changed?

_____
_____
_____
_____
_____
_____
_____
_____
_____
_____
_____
_____
_____

SECOND WEEK I CHOOSE

Worry is a misuse of imagination. —Dan Zadra

Take one of your impossible things, perhaps your favorite one, choose it, and use it to do this exercise.

No matter how far "out there" it may be, use it anyway.

In this exercise, we are stretching out our minds just as we do our bodies. We can't get past our habits by staying in the same mindset.

I Choose sheets are another vital tool for being mentally flexible.

Remind yourself how to do this by reviewing *Chapter Three*, the *I Choose* chapter in this workbook. Have fun with this!

(This might be where you grab a piece of scrap paper and start writing. It's possible this could go on for pages!)

I Choose This Impossible Thing:

Second Week Recap

Pat yourself on the back for making it this far in your workbook!

Starting a new habit and then sticking with it is hard. Acknowledge that to yourself.

Our human, old self, does not want to let go. It's going to do everything it can to distract us from changing.

When you notice this in yourself, try not to give this resistance more power by berating yourself for not being perfect.

Let it go. It's not you. Move on.

Instead, go back to your workbook. Fill in what you might have missed. Take a breath and begin again.

Be like a child that falls, laughs, and rises again.

That's you!

Let's review what we did this week.

- You spent seven days imagining seven impossible things.
- You meditated every day.
- You made a quality list of what you would feel

like if you were the tree that picked you.

•You chose your favorite imagination, thought about it, commented on it, and did an I Choose sheet using it as a jumping-off point.

Did you miss any of this?

Don't worry. Don't give up. Keep going.

If you are in a mastermind group, perhaps you all could set a way to check in daily to make sure you've done your imagining for the day.

If you don't have someone to do this with, set your own type of reminder!

I know you won't let yourself down, and if you do, you'll pick yourself up and keep on going. You know why?

Because you are an Imagination Master, that's why!

CHAPTER SEVEN: WEEK THREE

Imagination and creativity can change the world.
—Anonymous

PERCEPTION RULES

Before we begin our week, let's take a moment and briefly examine one of my favorite topics, perception.

There are two modes of perception—*state of mind* and *point of view*. Our point of view is what we believe to be true and want to be true.

It's what we intentionally, or unintentionally, use as the building blocks of our lives. However, points of view become ruts and habits if not consistently examined, and too often we become prisoners of our point of view.

In this course, we are stepping out of ruts by stretching our point of view into something that better aligns with the concept of an infinite Intelligence, a loving God, an abundant life.

This shift will open our self-imposed cell doors and begin to change our lives for the better.

If that were all it took, it would be fantastic.

But as I said, there are **two** modes of perception,

and they have to agree with each other.

Which means if we desire a permanent change, we also have to shift our state of mind perception.

State of mind refers to our emotions and feelings. It's what we *feel to be true*, either out of a form of joy or out of fear.

Guess which mode is stronger. You're right. It's the state of mind perception.

We can believe that God is good all we want, but if our internal emotions and feelings reside in either fear or doubt that it is true for us, our outside world will more closely match that state of mind rather than our point of view.

This need to align our perceptions is why I have added so many exercises like meditation, writing, and choosing in this course. To do these, we have to feel what we believe and want.

Once we get our state of mind perception in harmony with our point of view perception, we are in-sync, or in-flow with the universe.

Here's what we want to do. We want to bring our state of mind and point of view into harmony.

Until our emotions and feelings are the same as our point of view, it will be hard to make changes. And if we do succeed, it will be hard to do.

Why? Because we had to make it happen by fighting our hidden perceptions. When our perceptions aren't in harmony with each other, what we accomplish won't be as satisfying or as long-lasting.

Doing this work, we are not making anything happen. We are getting out of the way.

If you would like more about perception, my book *Living in Grace: The Shift To Spiritual Perception* lays the whole idea out in an easy to understand form.

My book *The Four Essential Questions: Choosing Spiritually Healthy Habits* looks at these two modes of perception in another way, with the focus of breaking out of limiting ruts and paradigms. Find these two books anywhere you get your books.

Welcome to your third week of Imagination Mastery! Are you settled into a routine for getting your daily imagination work done?

Are you using your quality words to see your life differently? Have you taken the time to put them in order? It's so important to do this.

Often in our lives, we make choices based on a preference that we think we have. Habits and expectations are easy to follow. Like taking the same road to work every day. But what if that isn't the best road for you to take?

Using your ordered quality words as a tool to make decisions will help break those habits and dissolve those expectations that don't fit who you are, or what you want.

If you are new to Quality Word lists, I Choose sheets, and meditation, then these new tools might feel strange at first. But eventually, you will discover they are incredibly useful tools to use in your daily life.

I mean, who doesn't need a hammer, a wrench, and a screwdriver in their house?

These tools are the same. Simple, easy to use, perfect for almost every situation.

However, like all tools, they only do you good if you use them.

PICK YOUR SYMBOL

This week you are going to pick an animal, although by now you might be aware that it is often the symbol that chooses you.

There is one other problem with picking an animal. It is so tempting to choose one that you already love, or you have a relationship with.

No. Not that one, even if it was the one that popped into your head. Instead, pause, listen again, and let it be something new.

Maybe it will be an animal that you don't even like or know anything about. It doesn't matter, go with that one.

Remember, this course is all about shifting locked in perceptions and points of view. Every animal has something to teach us, and qualities to share.

Something New!

We are adding one extra element to your imagination workbook. After the week is over, you are going to write a short imagination.

Notice that I didn't say a short story because I

don't want you to worry about the quality of what you are writing.

This is a short imagination. Perhaps include your bird, tree, or animal. Maybe use one of your imaginations as a jumping-off spot.

Whatever you use, don't worry about proper writing style, spelling, grammar, etc. This writing isn't for anyone but you. Perhaps one day it will grow into something more, but for now, it is a mind-stretching exercise.

Oh, and don't forget your meditation time. Maybe your animal will hang out with you, maybe under the tree, or in the tree with you, along with your bird.

Goodness, you are attracting quite a family, aren't you?

Enjoy your week!

WEEK THREE SET UP

The best use of imagination is creativity.
—Deepak Chopra

Today's Date:_____

Play with the idea of being your animal.

What does your animal do? How does it move?
How does it take care of its young?

Where does it live? Look up the symbol of your
animal, how does that relate to you?

This week I imagine myself to be this
animal:_____

How would you feel if you were this animal? Listen within to hear the answers. Try for ten qualities! (This is your unordered quality words list.)

1._____

2._____

3. _____

4. _____

5. _____

6. _____

7. _____

8. _____

9. _____

10. _____

My animal looks like this to me: (Go ahead. Draw, paste, scribble, your animal. No, it doesn't have to look like it. Don't judge, Play!)

Check back to *Chapter Two* on Quality Lists to remind yourself how to put these words in order and then how to use them.

My quality words in order for how I would feel if I were this animal.

1._____

2._____

3. _____

4. _____

5. _____

6. _____

7. _____

8. _____

9. _____

10. _____

Fantastic! Now that you have these qualities— use them. Imagine yourself as this animal this week instead of your ordinary self. Let this animal help you do your daily imaginations.

WEEK THREE: DAY ONE

Today's Date:_____

Today's Meditation Focus:_____

My Seven Impossible Things Before Breakfast.

1._____
_____

2._____
_____

3._____
_____

4._____
_____

5._____
_____

6._____
_____

7._____
_____

WEEK THREE: DAY TWO

Today's Date:_____

Today's Meditation Focus:_____

My Seven Impossible Things Before Breakfast.

1._____
_____

2._____
_____

3._____
_____

4._____
_____

5._____
_____

6._____
_____

7._____
_____

WEEK THREE: DAY THREE

Today's Date:_____

Today's Meditation Focus:_____

My Seven Impossible Things Before Breakfast.

1._____

_____

2._____

_____

3._____

_____

4._____

_____

5._____

_____

6._____

_____

7._____

_____

Week Three: Day Four

Today's Date:_____

Today's Meditation Focus:_____

My Seven Impossible Things Before Breakfast.

1._____
_____

2._____
_____

3._____
_____

4._____
_____

5._____
_____

6._____
_____

7._____
_____

WEEK THREE: DAY FIVE

Today's Date:_____

Today's Meditation Focus:_____

My Seven Impossible Things Before Breakfast.

1._____
_____

2._____
_____

3._____
_____

4._____
_____

5._____
_____

6._____
_____

7._____
_____

WEEK THREE: DAY SIX

Today's Date:_____

Today's Meditation Focus:_____

My Seven Impossible Things Before Breakfast.

1._____
_____

2._____
_____

3._____
_____

4._____
_____

5._____
_____

6._____
_____

7._____
_____

WEEK THREE: DAY SEVEN

Today's Date:_____

Today's Meditation Focus:_____

My Seven Impossible Things Before Breakfast.

1._____

_____

2._____

_____

3._____

_____

4._____

_____

5._____

_____

6._____

_____

7._____

_____

THIRD WEEK REVIEW

"Happiness is not an ideal of reason, but of imagination." —Immanuel Kant

Three weeks in, and things are changing. Have you noticed?

Did anything happen that surprised you this week?

What happened during your meditations? Are you forgetting to do them? Why? Just observe what happened.

Read the imagination story that you wrote. What does it tell you about yourself and the world around you?

This is all about awareness of what perceptions drive our reality, so that we can allow our lives to stretch into the infinite.

THIRD WEEK I CHOOSE

"The true sign of intelligence is not knowledge but imagination." —Albert Einstein

Take one of your impossible things, perhaps your favorite one, choose it, and use it to do this exercise.

No matter how far "out there" it may be, use it anyway.

In this exercise, we are stretching out our minds just as we do our bodies. We can't get past our habits by staying in the same mindset.

I Choose sheets are another vital tool for being mentally flexible.

Remind yourself how to do this by reviewing *Chapter Three*, the *I Choose* chapter in this workbook. Have fun with this!

(This might be where you grab a piece of scrap paper and start writing. It's possible this could go on for pages!)

I Choose This Impossible Thing:

_____

_____

_____

_____

Remember what we are doing is training ourselves to be aware of what we are thinking and doing. And then we are allowing our imaginations to bring us into unlimited possibilities.

My Favorite Impossible Thing For The Week:

_____
_____
_____
_____
_____

Things I noticed:

_____
_____
_____
_____

What has changed?

_____
_____
_____
_____
_____
_____
_____
_____
_____
_____

Here's your new assignment for the week:

Write a short imagination. Be your bird, tree, or animal. Or take one of your daily imaginations and write what would happen if it were true.

_____

_____

_____

_____

_____

_____

_____

_____

_____

_____

_____

_____

_____

_____

_____

_____

_____

_____

_____

_____

_____

_____

_____

Third Week Recap

Congratulations on keeping up with the Seven Impossible Imaginations every day. If you sometimes struggle with this, perhaps do them a different way.

Instead of writing them down in your workbook, write somewhere else. Or record them. Or draw them. The point is to imagine.

Why not imagine all the different ways you can do an assignment. Not just this one. What about "life" assignments. How can you do them differently, so they bring meaning and joy to you?

Did you also play with your animal? Maybe you rode on its back through the forest. Imagine. Anything.

Don't get serious.

Don't judge.

Let it flow. Let imagination use you for the Divine's purpose of being creative.

If you still struggle, pay attention to what is stopping you. Noticing it is the first step to resistance losing its power.

Let the play and joy of imagination transform your daily life and expect to experience and see things you have never seen or experienced before!

And let the imagination story you write at the end of each week tell itself to you. You will be surprised at what happens!

Here's what you did this week:

• You spent seven days imagining seven impossible things.

•You meditated every day.

•You made a quality list of what you would feel like if you were the animal that picked you.

•You chose your favorite imagination, thought about it, commented on it, and did an I Choose sheet using it as a jumping-off point.

•You wrote an imagination story.

It was a good week, wasn't it?

Chapter Eight: Week Four

Imagination is the true magic carpet.
—Norman Vincent Peale

Welcome to your fourth week of Imagination Mastery!

How did your short imagination writing go for you this week? Was it easy? Hard? Did you judge everything that you wrote or just let it flow?

As a fiction writer, I love the moments when I get into the story, and my imagination takes me away to someplace I have never been before. Even as you write these little "stories" for yourself, let that happen.

Leave the world as you think it is, and let that part of you that knows there is more open up.

As I have mentioned before, it's not about how good your imagination writing is, it's that you do it, and then let the doing of it transform you.

So even though writing your imagination does add a few extra minutes onto the last day of each week, take the time to do it.

Actually, it doesn't have to be at the end of the week. Any time you get an idea, flip to your page and start writing. Or write on your computer, or on your phone, or record it.

Whatever you way you choose to imagine, is the right way for you.

PICK YOUR SYMBOL

This week you are going to pick a stone.

What? A stone? Yes, a stone.

Stones are amazing. They were here on this Earth long before we arrived. They hold the history of our world. Maybe our universe.

It doesn't have to be a special stone, like a gemstone. It could be a rock in your garden or one that you picked up at the beach or a walk in the woods.

See if you can discover what kind of stone it is by searching the internet for information.

What are its qualities? What does it symbolize? Every stone has a story. Let it tell it to you.

You could even use the story of the stone for your imagination writing this week.

WEEK FOUR SET UP

*But, I nearly forgot you must close your eyes,
otherwise...you won't see anything.*
—Alice, Alice in Wonderland

Today's Date:_____

Play with the idea of being your stone. What would that feel like?

This week I imagine myself to be this stone:_____

How would you feel if you were this stone?
Listen within to hear the answers. Try for ten
qualities! (This is your unordered quality words list.)

1._____

2._____

3. _____

4. _____

5. _____

6. _____

7. _____

8. _____

9. _____

10. _____

My stone looks like this to me: (Go ahead. Draw,
paste, scribble, your stone. No, it doesn't have to
look like it. Don't judge, Play!)

Check back to *Chapter Two* on Quality Lists to remind yourself how to put these words in order and then how to use them.

My quality words in order for how I would feel if I were this stone.

1._____

2._____

3. _____

4. _____

5. _____

6. _____

7. _____

8. _____

9. _____

10. _____

Fantastic! Now that you have these qualities—use them. Imagine yourself as this stone this week instead of your ordinary self. Let this stone help you do your daily imaginations.

Week Four: Day One

Today's Date:_____

Today's Meditation Focus:_____

My Seven Impossible Things Before Breakfast.

1._____
_____

2._____
_____

3._____
_____

4._____
_____

5._____
_____

6._____
_____

7._____
_____

WEEK FOUR: DAY TWO

Today's Date:_____

Today's Meditation Focus:_____

My Seven Impossible Things Before Breakfast.

1._____

_____

2._____

_____

3._____

_____

4._____

_____

5._____

_____

6._____

_____

7._____

_____

WEEK FOUR: DAY THREE

Today's Date:_____

Today's Meditation Focus:_____

My Seven Impossible Things Before Breakfast.

1._____
_____

2._____
_____

3._____
_____

4._____
_____

5._____
_____

6._____
_____

7._____
_____

WEEK FOUR: DAY FOUR

Today's Date:_____

Today's Meditation Focus:_____

My Seven Impossible Things Before Breakfast.

1._____

_____

2._____

_____

3._____

_____

4._____

_____

5._____

_____

6._____

_____

7._____

_____

WEEK FOUR: DAY FIVE

Today's Date:_____

Today's Meditation Focus:_____

My Seven Impossible Things Before Breakfast.

1._____
_____

2._____
_____

3._____
_____

4._____
_____

5._____
_____

6._____
_____

7._____
_____

WEEK FOUR: DAY SIX

Today's Date:_____

Today's Meditation Focus:_____

My Seven Impossible Things Before Breakfast.

1._____

_____

2._____

_____

3._____

_____

4._____

_____

5._____

_____

6._____

_____

7._____

_____

WEEK FOUR: DAY SEVEN

Today's Date:_____

Today's Meditation Focus:_____

My Seven Impossible Things Before Breakfast.

1._____

_____

2._____

_____

3._____

_____

4._____

_____

5._____

_____

6._____

_____

7._____

_____

Fourth Week Review

Imagination takes you everywhere.
—Anonymous

You did it! You completed your fourth week. Stand in front of the mirror and thank yourself for showing up.

I'm not kidding. Really. Go do it. How about doing it right now. I'll wait.

It was weird, wasn't it? But empowering. You can trust yourself to do what you said you would do.

I know there will be times you won't, but every time you do, it strengthens that muscle.

Imagine that you can show up for yourself all the time. What would that feel like?

Pretty good, right? It will only get better, so keep going!

FOURTH WEEK I CHOOSE

Imagination creates reality.
—Richard Wagner

Take one of your impossible things, perhaps your favorite one, choose it, and use it to do this exercise.

No matter how far "out there" it may be, use it anyway.

In this exercise, we are stretching out our minds just as we do our bodies. We can't get past our habits by staying in the same mindset.

I Choose sheets are another vital tool for being mentally flexible.

Remind yourself how to do this by reviewing *Chapter Three,* the *I Choose* chapter in this workbook. Have fun with this!

(This might be where you grab a piece of scrap paper and start writing. It's possible this could go on for pages!)

I Choose This Impossible Thing:

_____
_____
_____
_____

Remember what we are doing is training ourselves to be aware of what we are thinking and doing. And then we are allowing our imaginations to bring us into unlimited possibilities.

My Favorite Impossible Thing For The Week:

Things I noticed:

What has changed?

Write a short imagination. Be your bird, tree, animal, or stone. Or take one of your daily imaginations and write what would happen if it were true.

_____

_____

_____

_____

_____

_____

_____

_____

_____

_____

_____

_____

_____

_____

_____

_____

_____

_____

_____

_____

_____

_____

_____

Fourth Week Recap

The only limit to your impact is your imagination and commitment.
—Tony Robbins

What did you and your stone do this week?

What information did you learn from it?

Perhaps patience?

Or the use of pressure and "hard times" to transform you and your life into something that shines.

It's been a busy week. Here's what you did:

• You spent seven days imagining seven impossible things.
•You meditated every day.
•You made a quality list of what you would feel like if you were the stone that picked you.
•You chose your favorite imagination, thought about it, commented on it, and did an I Choose sheet using it as a jumping-off point.
•You wrote an imagination story.

You are over halfway through. Things are changing, aren't they?

CHAPTER NINE: WEEK FIVE

Imagination is an instrument of survival.
—Rogier Van Der Heide

Welcome to your fifth week of Imagination Mastery!

Perhaps by now doing imagination work every day has become part of your routine.

But if not, don't worry about it. Don't allow that mean voice in your head to berate you for what you haven't done. Instead, start now, even if you have to begin in the fifth week. Just start. Or go back and begin again. It's okay to start over.

The hardest part of doing anything is showing up. No one is judging your imaginations, or writing, or habits. So don't do it to yourself.

Just show up for yourself over and over again until the showing up part becomes part of your nature. Everything will evolve from there.

Use the tools that you are learning to be present for yourself. Perhaps do an I Choose sheet that begins with something like—*I choose to show up for myself.* Or this one—*I trust to do what is right for me.* Or the simple version, *I trust myself.*

The results might surprise you.

Pick Your Symbol

This week you are going to pick a flower. This one should feel pretty good. Who doesn't want to be a flower?

Are you going to be a flower you know or a new one? What does it mean to you? Why?

Remember it doesn't have to be a showy flower.

What about the tiny flowers we walk on without noticing? Or the ones that spread fragrance in the air but their blooms are barely noticeable.

Of course, there are the ones that spark our gardens into something spectacular. How do they do that?

Where does your flower like to grow? How many of its qualities can you find within yourself?

What does this flower symbolize to you? To the world?

Enjoy the idea of flowers this week. Let it be a beautiful one.

WEEK FIVE SET UP

What is now proved was once only imagined.
—*William Blake*

Today's Date:_____

Play with the idea of being your flower. What would that feel like?

This week I imagine myself to be this flower:_____

How would you feel if you were this flower?
Listen within to hear the answers. Try for ten
qualities! (This is your unordered quality words list.)

1._____

2._____

3. _____

4. _____

5. _____

6. _____

7. _____

8. _____

9. _____

10. _____

My flower look like this to me: (Go ahead.
Draw, paste, scribble, your flower. No, it doesn't
have to look like it. Don't judge, Play!)

Check back to *Chapter Two* on Quality Lists to remind yourself how to put these words in order and then how to use them.

My quality words in order for how I would feel if I were this flower.

1._____

2._____

3. _____

4. _____

5. _____

6. _____

7. _____

8. _____

9. _____

10. _____

Fantastic! Now that you have these qualities— use them. Imagine yourself as this flower this week instead of your ordinary self. Let your flower help you do your daily imaginations.

Week Five: Day One

Today's Date:_____

Today's Meditation Focus:_____

My Seven Impossible Things Before Breakfast.

1._____
_____

2._____
_____

3._____
_____

4._____
_____

5._____
_____

6._____
_____

7._____
_____

WEEK FIVE DAY TWO

Today's Date:_____

Today's Meditation Focus:_____

My Seven Impossible Things Before Breakfast.

1._____
_____

2._____
_____

3._____
_____

4._____
_____

5._____
_____

6._____
_____

7._____
_____

WEEK FIVE: DAY THREE

Today's Date:_____

Today's Meditation Focus:_____

My Seven Impossible Things Before Breakfast.

1._____
_____

2._____
_____

3._____
_____

4._____
_____

5._____
_____

6._____
_____

7._____
_____

Week Five: Day Four

Today's Date:_____

Today's Meditation Focus:_____

My Seven Impossible Things Before Breakfast.

1._____
_____

2._____
_____

3._____
_____

4._____
_____

5._____
_____

6._____
_____

7._____
_____

Week Five: Day Five

Today's Date:_____

Today's Meditation Focus:_____

My Seven Impossible Things Before Breakfast.

1._____
_____

2._____
_____

3._____
_____

4._____
_____

5._____
_____

6._____
_____

7._____
_____

WEEK FIVE: DAY SIX

Today's Date:_____

Today's Meditation Focus:_____

My Seven Impossible Things Before Breakfast.

1._____
_____

2._____
_____

3._____
_____

4._____
_____

5._____
_____

6._____
_____

7._____
_____

WEEK FIVE: DAY SEVEN

Today's Date:_____

Today's Meditation Focus:_____

My Seven Impossible Things Before Breakfast.

1._____

_____

2._____

_____

3._____

_____

4._____

_____

5._____

_____

6._____

_____

7._____

_____

FIFTH WEEK REVIEW

When one paints an ideal, one does not need to limit one's imagination. —Ellen Key

Congratulations! You completed your fifth week of being an Imagination Master.

I hope you are as proud of yourself as I am of you. By now, things should be moving around in your life enough to see that this simple idea changes lives.

If you are working with a friend or a group, this may be an excellent week to pause and appreciate the power of community.

If you are doing this by yourself, you are still in a community.

There are hundreds, maybe thousands, of other people doing this course, too. Imagine that they are present for you, as you are for them.

You are always being watched over.

How do I know?

Because we are all connected, we are all an integral essence of the One Divine Intelligence.

Imagine that!

FIFTH WEEK I CHOOSE

To raise new questions, new possibilities, to regard old problems from a new angle, requires creative imagination and marks real advance in science.
—Albert Einstein

Take one of your impossible things, perhaps your favorite one, and choose it use it to do this exercise.

No matter how far "out there" it may be, use it anyway.

In this exercise, we are stretching out our minds just as we do our bodies. We can't get past our habits by staying in the same mindset.

I Choose sheets are another vital tool for being mentally flexible.

Remind yourself how to do this by reviewing *Chapter Three*, the *I Choose* chapter in this workbook. Have fun with this!

(It's possible this could go on for pages!)

I Choose This Impossible Thing:

_____
_____
_____
_____

Remember what we are doing is training ourselves to be aware of what we are thinking and doing. And then we are allowing our imaginations to bring us into unlimited possibilities.

My Favorite Impossible Thing For The Week:

Things I noticed:

What has changed?

Write a short imagination. Be your bird, tree, animal, stone, or flower. Or take one of your daily imaginations and write what would happen if it were true.

_____

_____

_____

_____

_____

_____

_____

_____

_____

_____

_____

_____

_____

_____

_____

_____

_____

_____

_____

_____

_____

_____

_____

_____

_____

Fifth Week Recap

Now that we are at the end of the fifth week, don't forget to spend some time with your imagination story.

You can write, draw, or speak into a recorder an imagination about the five elements you have imagined yourself to be so far.

You've been a been bird, tree, animal, stone, and flower.

See, you've been many parts of nature. Has it inspired you to take a walk, or sit in nature more?

Perhaps do your meditation in nature. Feel what it is sharing with you. Rest in the fact that you are always part of this Oneness.

Here's what you did this week:

• You spent seven days imagining seven impossible things.
•You meditated every day.
•You made a quality list of what you would feel like if you were the flower that picked you.
•You chose your favorite imagination, thought about it, commented on it, and did an I Choose sheet using it as a jumping-off point.
•You wrote an imagination story.

Here we go... Week six coming up

CHAPTER TEN: WEEK SIX

Reality leaves a lot to the imagination. —John Lennon

Welcome to week six of Imagination Mastery

If you are here, congratulations, you rock!

Now that you are truly becoming an Imagination Master, don't forget you can do these assignments in whatever way works for you.

This workbook is a guide, not a rule.

Let your imagination run wild. Imagining won't hurt anyone or anything, as long as you always begin with the intent to be—and do—good.

If for some reason temptation snuck in to imagine bad things, don't go there.

That's the what-if of worry, or revenge, or competition, or winning at someone else's expense.

No matter what, don't let that imagination take over. Although it may look as though some people get away with that kind of behavior, it won't last, and no matter what they say, they are not happy.

Stay in the lane of choosing the best for everyone. Don't let the claim of being better than someone else remove you from the joy of experiencing infinite Love.

We all are tempted sometimes. And sometimes, we make the mistake of succumbing to that temptation.

But we can all come back, and be stronger for it. Imagine yourself, and everyone that your thoughts rest upon, as a child of the Divine. Imagine that and all will be well.

PICK YOUR SYMBOL

This week you are going to imagine yourself having at least one superpower. You can keep that superpower all week, or change it daily, or even twice a day.

Do you think that you have no idea what superpower you would choose?

You know I don't believe that. I believe that all of us harbor a desire to be more, have magic, do things we can't normally do.

Movies and TV shows filled with people with superpowers are everywhere. That's because it taps into all our desires.

So go ahead. Have a superpower. Imagine using it in your daily life. What would you do with it?

That's what you are going to imagine each day!

Let yourself feel child-like, open to imagination, and the joy it brings.

At the end of the week, write, draw, speak into a recorder, an imagination about you with your super, or magical, powers.

WEEK SIX SET UP

Imagination will often carry us to worlds that never were. But without it we go nowhere.
—Carl Sagan

Today's Date:_____

Play with the idea of having a super power and or being magical.

Perhaps you are a wizard? Or a shapeshifter?

What would that feel like? What could you do? How would you live life differently?

This week I imagine myself to have this superpower:_____

How would you feel if you were this superpower? Listen within to hear the answers. Try for ten qualities! (This is your unordered quality words list.)

1._____

2._____

3. _____

4. _____

5. _____

6. _____

7. _____

8. _____

9. _____

10. _____

My superpower feels—or looks—like this to me: (Go ahead. Draw, paste, scribble, your superpower. No, it doesn't have to look like it. Don't judge, Play!)

Check back to *Chapter Two* on Quality Lists to remind yourself how to put these words in order and then how to use them.

My quality words in order for how I would feel if I were this superpower.

1._____

2._____

3. _____

4. _____

5. _____

6. _____

7. _____

8. _____

9. _____

10. _____

Fantastic! Now that you have these qualities— use them. Imagine yourself as this superpower this week instead of your ordinary self. Let your superpower help you do your daily imaginations.

WEEK SIX: DAY ONE

Today's Date:_____

I have this superpower:_____

Seven Things I Could Do With It.

1._____
_____

2._____
_____

3._____
_____

4._____
_____

5._____
_____

6._____
_____

7._____
_____

Week Six Day Two

Today's Date:_____

I have this superpower:_____

Seven Things I Could Do With It.

1._____
_____

2._____
_____

3._____
_____

4._____
_____

5._____
_____

6._____
_____

7._____
_____

WEEK SIX: DAY THREE

Today's Date:_____

I have this superpower:_____

Seven Things I Could Do With It.

1._____
_____

2._____
_____

3._____
_____

4._____
_____

5._____
_____

6._____
_____

7._____
_____

Week Six: Day Four

Today's Date:_____

I have this superpower:_____

Seven Things I Could Do With It.

1._____
_____

2._____
_____

3._____
_____

4._____
_____

5._____
_____

6._____
_____

7._____
_____

WEEK SIX: DAY FIVE

Today's Date:_____

I have this superpower:_____

Seven Things I Could Do With It.

1._____
_____

2._____
_____

3._____
_____

4._____
_____

5._____
_____

6._____
_____

7._____
_____

WEEK SIX: DAY SIX

Today's Date:_____

I have this superpower:_____

Seven Things I Could Do With It.

1._____
_____

2._____
_____

3._____
_____

4._____
_____

5._____
_____

6._____
_____

7._____
_____

WEEK SIX: DAY SEVEN

Today's Date:_____

I have this superpower:_____

Seven Things I Could Do With It.

1._____
_____

2._____
_____

3._____
_____

4._____
_____

5._____
_____

6._____
_____

7._____
_____

Sixth Week Review

If you can imagine it, you can achieve it. If you can dream it, you can become it.
—William Arthur Ward

Phew. Six weeks wrapped up and finished!

Do you realize that you have written two-hundred and ninety-four imaginations?

Plus you have added into your life at least one superpower. Maybe more.

Imagine that!

You did this by doing one day at a time. Steady. No rushing.

This is how things that last are accomplished.

And you have cracked the code.

Congratulations!

Sixth Week I Choose

The world is but a canvas to the imagination.
—Thoreau

Take one of your impossible things, perhaps your favorite one, choose it, and use it to do this exercise.

No matter how far "out there" it may be, use it anyway.

In this exercise, we are stretching out our minds just as we do our bodies. We can't get past our habits by staying in the same mindset.

I Choose sheets are another vital tool for being mentally flexible.

Remind yourself how to do this by reviewing *Chapter Three*, the *I Choose* chapter in this workbook. Have fun with this!

(It's possible this could go on for pages!)

I Choose This Impossible Thing:

_____
_____
_____
_____
_ _____

Remember what we are doing is training ourselves to be aware of what we are thinking and doing. And then we are allowing our imaginations to bring us into unlimited possibilities.

My Favorite Impossible Thing For The Week:

Things I noticed:

What has changed?

Write a short imagination about being your superpower. Perhaps add in your bird, tree, animal, stone, or flower. Or take one of your daily imaginations and write what would happen if it were true.

_____

_____

_____

_____

_____

_____

_____

_____

_____

_____

_____

_____

_____

_____

_____

_____

_____

_____

_____

_____

_____

_____

_____

_____

_____

SIXTH WEEK RECAP

Superpowers are fantastic. Being magical is lovely.

But doing what we say we are going to do has more power than all of that.

So if you are here, you already have a superpower —the ability to keep going in spite of temptations, distractions, distress, or even success.

You have kept a promise to yourself. There is magic in that!

Here's what you did this week:

•You spent seven days imagining having superpowers.
•You meditated every day.
•You made a quality list of what you would feel like if you were that superpower that picked you.
•You chose your favorite imagination, thought about it, commented on it, and did an I Choose sheet using it as a jumping-off point.
•You wrote an imagination story.

Just one week to go. And because I know how much fun having superpowers can be, we'll continue with that for one more week, and then we'll wrap it up and see what we have done.

If you have a habit of stopping before you finish something, notice that, and keep going. Finish this.

Trust yourself to do what you promise yourself that you will do.

Ready? Let's go!

CHAPTER ELEVEN: WEEK SEVEN

Anyone who lives within their means suffers from a lack of imagination.
—Oscar Wilde

Although unplanned by me, our seventh week landed on the eleventh chapter. There are always signs and symbols waiting for us and I love this one.

What do these two mean?

Number seven is considered the number for completion, and eleven is often associated with moving from personal power to spiritual power.

Perfect, right?

Because after this week, you will have completed seven weeks of imagination, and that has moved you from thinking you are in charge and into more of an acceptance that the Divine is in charge.

As we erase our biases and locked in perceptions, we experience more of that Reality as the doors of our perception open into the Infinite.

Take this last week and luxuriate in the opportunity to do this kind of work.

It's an opportunity to shift your life by doing nothing more than shifting your perceptions and then following the residual guidance into what you do with your daily life.

PICK YOUR SYMBOL

This week we are staying with superpowers. Try out a few different ones. Perhaps, ones you might never have thought of before.

What if you could make yourself as small as an ant, or as large as a building? What if when you blinked, the world changed colors, or you waved your hand, and everything stood still except you.

For your seven impossible things every day you'll be imagining what you could do with your superpowers.

How would you change your world?

Have fun—no judgment or listening to the mean voice in your head. Ever. But this week I have your attention, so I can remind you.

Play!

Let the Divine creative force move through you this week.

Imagine how that feels and flow with it.

WEEK SEVEN SET UP

Imagination is the beginning of creation. You imagine what you desire, you will what you imagine, and at last, you create what you will.
—George Bernard Shaw

Today's Date:_____

Play with the idea of having a super power and or being magical.

Perhaps you are a wizard? Or a shapeshifter?

What would that feel like? What could you do? How would you live life differently?

This week I imagine myself to have this superpower:_____

How would you feel if you were this superpower? Listen within to hear the answers. Try for ten qualities! (This is your unordered quality words list.)

1._____

2._____

3. _____

4. _____

5. _____

6. _____

7. _____

8. _____

9. _____

10. _____

My superpower feels—or looks—like this to me: (Go ahead. Draw, paste, scribble, your superpower. No, it doesn't have to look like it. Don't judge, Play!)

Check back to *Chapter Two* on Quality Lists to remind yourself how to put these words in order and then how to use them.

My quality words in order for how I would feel if I were this superpower.

1._____

2._____

3. _____

4. _____

5. _____

6. _____

7. _____

8. _____

9. _____

10. _____

Fantastic! Now that you have these qualities—use them. Imagine yourself as this superpower this week instead of your ordinary self. Let your superpower help you do your daily imaginations.

WEEK SEVEN: DAY ONE

Today's Date:_____

I have this superpower:_____

Seven Things I Could Do With It.

1._____
_____

2._____
_____

3._____
_____

4._____
_____

5._____
_____

6._____
_____

7._____
_____

Week Seven Day Two

Today's Date:_____

I have this superpower:_____

Seven Things I Could Do With It.

1._____

_____

2._____

_____

3._____

_____

4._____

_____

5._____

_____

6._____

_____

7._____

_____

Week Seven: Day Three

Today's Date:_____

I have this superpower:_____

Seven Things I Could Do With It.

1._____
_____

2._____
_____

3._____
_____

4._____
_____

5._____
_____

6._____
_____

7._____
_____

WEEK SEVEN: DAY FOUR

Today's Date:_____

I have this superpower:_____

Seven Things I Could Do With It.

1._____
_____

2._____
_____

3._____
_____

4._____
_____

5._____
_____

6._____
_____

7._____
_____

WEEK SEVEN: DAY FIVE

Today's Date:_____

I have this superpower:_____

Seven Things I Could Do With It.

1._____
_____

2._____
_____

3._____
_____

4._____
_____

5._____
_____

6._____
_____

7._____
_____

WEEK SEVEN: DAY SIX

Today's Date:_____

I have this superpower:_____

Seven Things I Could Do With It.

1._____
_____

2._____
_____

3._____
_____

4._____
_____

5._____
_____

6._____
_____

7._____
_____

Week Seven: Day Seven

Today's Date:_____

I have this superpower:_____

Seven Things I Could Do With It.

1._____
_____

2._____
_____

3._____
_____

4._____
_____

5._____
_____

6._____
_____

7._____
_____

SEVENTH WEEK REVIEW

Reality can be beaten with enough imagination.
—Mark Twain

Since we are in our seventh, and final week, we have a slightly different review.

It involves all those quality word lists that you have done these last seven weeks.

You are going to take the top word from each of your ordered lists and *bring them into one quality word list.*

If you have duplicates, don't put them in twice. Instead, use the word below that in this master list.

At the same time, make a separate list of the duplicate words. In a minute, we are going to do something with both those lists. But, like all quality word lists, they are first unordered and then they must be ordered.

There only a few more things to do. Remember how good completion feels.

Enjoy doing this. It's like designing the blueprint of the "house" you want to live in from now on.

Do the lists, then we'll talk about how to use them, at the end of the chapter.

This is your unordered list of the top quality words from the last seven weeks.

1._____

2._____

3. _____

4. _____

5. _____

6. _____

7. _____

This is your ordered list of the top quality words from the last seven weeks.

1._____

2._____

3. _____

4. _____

5. _____

6. _____

7. _____

This is your unordered list of the duplicate words from the past seven weeks.

1._____

2._____

3. _____

4. _____

5. _____

6. _____

7. _____

This is your ordered list of the duplicate words from the past seven weeks,

1._____

2._____

3. _____

4. _____

5. _____

6. _____

7. _____

Seventh Week I Choose

Imagination is the power of the mind over the possibilities of things.
—William Stevens

Yes, one last I Choose sheet.

You have seven weeks of things from which to choose.

You could always go back and re-choose something you chose before.

After all, you are different now.

Or choose something new. By now, I Choose sheets are second nature for you.

You can write them on scraps of paper, on the paper placemat at the restaurant while you wait for your food, or say them into a recorder.

Do them in a way that works for you, but do them!

Consciously choosing is one of the most powerful things that we can do.

Sometimes it feels like life, and the world is choosing for us. Here's your chance to change that.

I Choose This Impossible Thing:

_____
_____
_____
_____
_ _____

My Current Favorite Impossible Thing:

_____
_____
_____
_____
_____

Things I noticed:

_____
_____
_____
_____

What has changed?

_____
_____
_____
_____
_____
_____
_____
_____

Here's your last imagination. It is your chance to imagine something you have never imagined before. Be something other than yourself. Let your imagination run wild.

We live in an infinitely expanding universe. There is no reason to keep ourselves inside of a story that is limiting in any way. No one will know what you write here unless you want to share. Let joy and goodness lead the way. Imagine that!

_____
_____
_____
_____
_____
_____
_____
_____
_____
_____
_____
_____
_____
_____
_____
_____
_____
_____
_____
_____
_____
_____
_____
_____

RECAP

Bring ideas in and entertain them royally, for one of them may be the king.
—Mark Van Doren

You did it!

You completed seven weeks of imagining! As a result, your outside life is changing.

Have you noticed? It had to have happened because when **you** change, so does your life.

All you have to do is notice, and celebrate it, and then keep practicing.

But before we end our seven weeks together, we have those last two quality lists to discuss.

We can't leave them out because they are like the treasure at the end of the rainbow.

These last two quality lists can travel with you for the rest of your life.

Or you can replace, or add to them if you do this class again. As you change, evolve, see things differently, your lists may change.

Just like we can turn around when we realize we are on a journey to a destination we don't want, we can do that in life, too.

But we need a place to start.

So, yes, you can do this course over and over again. You can take time off or immediately begin again.

But for now, let's talk about what to do with your ordered quality words that ended up on your master list.

Obviously, they mean a great deal to you. Because with all the quality words vital to you, the ones on this list made the top seven.

What does that mean to you?

It means that by using these quality words as guides, you can now consciously choose what you want to experience in life.

Here are two examples of what that might mean:

It might mean you change the chairs in your living room because *comfortable* is the top word on your master list, and although the chairs are beautiful, they are not comfortable.

Or perhaps the top word on your list is valued.

If so, that might mean you need to examine your relationships to discover if they value you. (I mean it. You have to. Now that you are conscious of what you desire, you can't ignore it.)

If they don't, why not? Pay attention. Is it them, or you?

Did you think you don't deserve more, or are they unwilling, or incapable of valuing you? Maybe it's a mix of both.

No matter. Now you can choose consciously.

Do you want to stay unvalued? Of course not.

So you can do an I Choose sheet that begins with something like, *I choose to be valued.* Then release all the reasons why you block yourself from feeling valued.

If you still aren't being valued, then you can choose to let go of those relationships or jobs. Sometimes, by doing this work, this kind of thing takes care of itself. Other times you will need to take action.

What's important is that you take this Master Quality List seriously. It is the key to transforming your life to match who you are and what you desire.

Go through the how-to-use the list in *Chapter Two* again, and follow the four steps outlined there.

I can make you a promise that if you do this work, things will change in the direction of your conscious intent.

If I had told you that this Imagination Mastery book is a class in learning how to be a wizard or a magician, then no matter how much work it entailed, you probably would have agreed it was worth it.

Well, these simple things do work like "magic."

Not because we are breaking any laws of the universe, but because we are tapping into the one that can't be altered.

What you perceive to be reality magnifies.

In the Enneagram, The Stages of the Work, it's stated slightly differently,—"If you were transformed, the world would be transformed."—but it's the same.

Now for the second list that you made.

This is the list of the duplicate words. I think you already know why I had you separate them from your Master List.

These qualities are more than important to you, they are essential. So much so, that they ended up at the top of more than one list.

Ask yourself if you are honoring your basic life needs represented by these quality words.

Have you, and are you, designing your life around them? Or are you ignoring them? If so, you are doing it at the risk of your own unhappiness.

But I know you aren't going to do that anymore. You are an Imagination Master, and you have the tools at your fingertips to help you with whatever you need to do.

Let's say that the top quality on your duplicate list is love.

The word love is so all-encompassing that it needs more of your attention. What kind of love? From whom? In what way?

It would be a fantastic idea to do a quality word list for the way that you would feel if you were experiencing the kind of love you meant when you chose that word.

Then, you will have a clearer idea of what you want love to be like in your life.

Clarity and conscious choosing are imperative.

What if by the quality love you mean you would like to spend more time with your family but to feel more valued at work, you work harder.

Or you believe that your family needs the money more than time with you? Are these beliefs undermining the quality of love in your family?

By becoming clear about what you want and

putting your quality words at the forefront of your choices, everything begins to work together in harmony.

I could go on and on about the importance of this work, and how to use it.

That's why I have written more books on the subject. So perhaps pick up one of those books, if you would like to learn more.

But for now, not to worry.

What you are doing within this *Imagination Mastery* book will transform your experience of life, if you let it.

Let me know if I can help.

~ Beca

Go confidently in the direction of your dreams, and live the life you have imagined.
—Henry David Thoreau

PS
As I mentioned, this book is part of *The Shift Series*. If you love the concepts and want to learn more about them, you will find them laid out in different ways in the other books.

When you join my mailing list, I'll give you one of The Shift Series books for free, *The Daily Shift*.

This book is packed with seven-day practice sessions for everything from money, health, or love. So many you can practice for over half a year, before repeating yourself.

Join me here: becalewis.com/spiritual-self-help

Plus, I often run contests, and if you are on the list, you might be a lucky winner!

Plus, I am looking forward to getting to know you!

AND don't forget to get your free worksheets for the book here: becalewis.com/imagination

Here's The Shift Series current list:

•*Living in Grace*: The Shift to Spiritual Perception
•*The 4 Essential Questions*: Choosing Spiritually Healthy Habits
•*The 28 Day Shift To Wealth*: A Daily Prosperity Plan
•*The Intent Course*: Say Yes To What Moves You
•*The Daily Shift*: Daily Lessons From Love To Money
•*Imagination Mastery:* A Workbook For Shifting Your Reality

ACKNOWLEDGMENTS

My heartfelt thanks to the *Imagination Mastery* class for being the beta testers for this book.

And for those wonderful members of the Beca Book Community who checked this book (and so many more) for accuracy.

Thank you especially to Jet Tucker and Jamie Lewis for cleaning up all my errors, and always being there when I need them to check up on me.

More Ways To Connect:

Connect with me online:

http://www.facebook.com/becalewiscreative
https://www.facebook.com/groups/becalewisfans/
http://instagram.com/becalewis
http://www.linkedin.com/in/becalewis
https://www.goodreads.com/BecaLewis
http://www.pinterest.com/theshift/
http://www.twitter.com/becalewis
http://www.facebook.com/becalewis

ABOUT BECA LEWIS

Beca writes books that she hopes will change people's perceptions of themselves and the world, and open possibilities to things and ideas that are waiting to be seen and experienced.

At sixteen, Beca founded her own dance studio. Later, she received a Master's Degree in Dance in Choreography from UCLA and founded the Harbinger Dance Theatre, a multimedia dance company, while continuing to run her dance school.

After graduating—to better support her three children—Beca switched to the sales field, where she worked as an employee and independent contractor to many industries, excelling in each while perfecting and teaching her Shift® system, and writing books.

She joined the financial industry in 1983 and became an Associate Vice President of Investments at a major stock brokerage firm, and was a licensed Certified Financial Planner for more than twenty years.

This diversity, along with a variety of life challenges, helped fuel the desire to share what she's learned by writing and talking with the hope that it will make a difference in other people's lives.

Beca grew up in State College, PA, with the dream of becoming a dancer and then a writer. She carried that dream forward as she fulfilled a childhood wish by moving to Southern California in 1969. Beca told her family she would never move back to the cold.

After living there for thirty years, she met

her husband Delbert Lee Piper, Sr., at a retreat in Virginia, and everything changed. They decided to find a place they could call their own which sent them off traveling around the United States. For a year or so they lived and worked in a few different places before returning to live in the cold once again near Del's family in a small town in Northeast Ohio, not too far from State College.

When not working and teaching together, they love to visit and play with their combined family of eight children and five grandchildren, read, study, do yoga or taiji, feed birds, work in their garden, and design things. Actually, designing things is what Beca loves to do. Del enjoys the end result.

Made in the USA
Middletown, DE
21 July 2020